Table of Cor

MW01484538

# Build Credit to Build Wealth

## The Blueprint for a Wealthy Credit Score

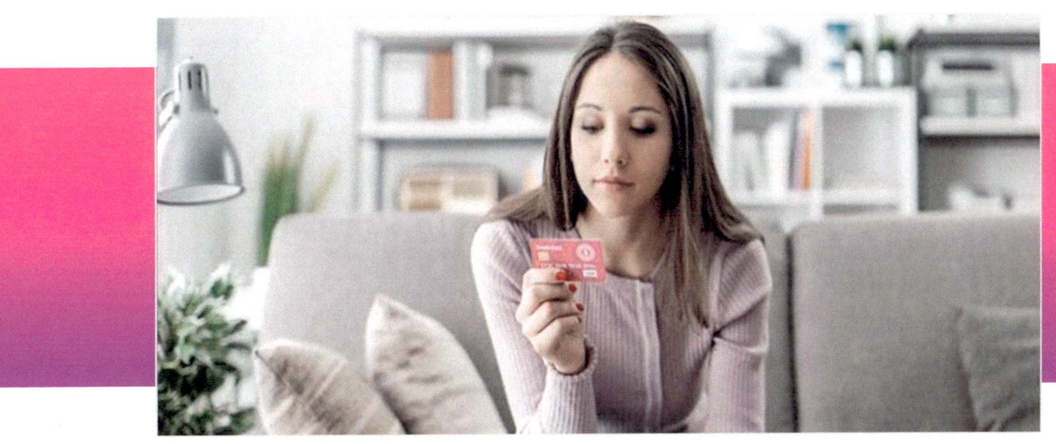

If you've read the book "*Keeping Score* – What You Need to Know to Make Your Credit Score Grow", you should have a good idea of what credit is, how credit works, tips & tricks on improving your credit. It has helped thousands understand it, improve it and get in position to start their journey to wealth building. I, myself spent thousands of dollars on credit repair companies to restore my credit when there were secrets that I hadn't heard of, things I could've done myself to obtain optimal credit. This workbook gives you the step by step instructions, credits tips & secrets all in one place.

My life's mission is to introduce everyday people to wealth building opportunities. One of the most critical pieces to building wealth is having good credit. Of the thousands of individuals I have helped become homeowners, a great amount did not understand the value of credit or how to decipher a credit report. It's the boogeyman in the closet that no one wants to deal with. What they don't understand is that its not as hard or scary to understand as they think.

If you follow the instructions and do the homework assignments in this workbook, you should be well on your way to having great credit scores within a matter of months. The steps here have proven successful time & time again.

# Setting Goals

**What** does success look like to you? Is it a promotion, starting a business, or increasing your credit score? The best way to ensure you are successful (whatever that means to you) is by creating attainable goals and sticking to them. There is a formula to successful goal setting. Your goals should be specific, measurable, achievable, realistic, and time-based. Here are the 5 steps to ensure your goals are met:

- ✓ Think it
- ✓ Write it
- ✓ Speak it
- ✓ Work it
- ✓ Receive it

**Dream/Think/Visualize** your goals. Whatever it is you want, it must first be a thought. Close your eyes and imagine where you want to be in a year (or whatever your timeframe is). Imagine what you will be doing, what you will be wearing, your attitude, your gratitude, what your life will be like. Visualize it as if it were you today and meditate on it daily.

**Write** down your goals. Habakkuk 2:2 says write down the vision & make it plain. Create a vision board and place it on your wall. Write down your goals in your phone and look at them daily. They are highlights of things you have accomplished and reminders of things you still need to do. They are your guide. Keep them forever and look back at them. You will be amazed by all your goals that you have conquered.

**Speak** your goals daily. Affirm-Declare-Decree. Whether you speak negatively or positively, something happens in the universe. Speak life! Because life & death are in the power of the tongue. Open your goals in your phone and speak them out loud every morning before you start your day. Start with I will...

**Embody/Work** your goals. If you want a 700-credit score, what does that take? How about a new job? If that means getting the necessary training, doing the necessary networking, paying down your bills little by little. You can't expect the work to happen by itself. Yes! Thinking, writing, and speaking are vehicles, but embodying is the gas that's going to get you to your destination

**Receive it.** When you've done those 4 things sequentially, Manifestation will occur. It's the harvest of all your hard work. The 6-figure income, the 25lb weight loss, the 770-credit score, the new car, the beautiful home. Its whatever success looks like to you.

## Monitoring Your Credit Report

Monitoring your credit report is essential to gain & maintain excellent credit health. It's like getting checkups from the Doctor. If you've ever faced a major health issue, the Doctor will tell you to come back every so often to monitor the issue to ensure it doesn't come back or get worse. And if something does occur, you can address it, attack it, and hopefully get cured of it in the early stages. It's the same thing with credit. If you're not monitoring it, something can sneak on your credit report, wreak havoc and potentially destroy your life.

# Notes

# Reading Your Credit Report

While there are many credit monitoring platforms, one of my favorites is Credit Karma. If you've read the book, *Keeping Score*, you already know that Credit Karma credit scores are not FICO scores. These scores aren't helpful in determining your credit worthiness for purchasing a home. However, the credit information on Credit Karma is useful in measuring movement & changes with your credit & score, and seeing your overall credit picture.

We will use both Credit Karma & AnnualCreditReport.com to guide you with comprehensive steps to optimize your credit. With Credit Karma, you can monitor your credit monthly and watch the progression (or regression) of your credit score & profile. While Annualcreditreport.com simply provides a free credit report once a year with no monthly monitoring involved. It is useful as it includes all three credit bureaus, while Credit Karma only provides Transunion & Equifax.

**Sign up or log in to Credit Karma (www.creditkarma.com)**

credit karma

Diagram A

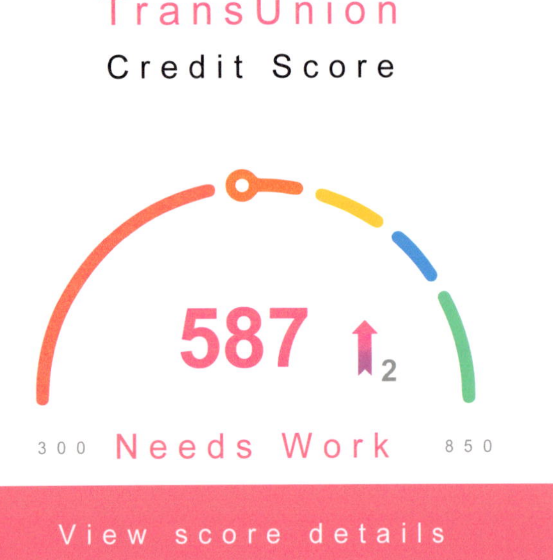


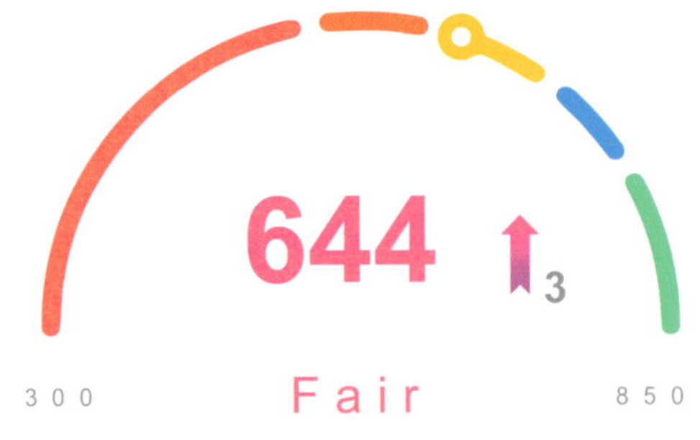

# Notes

# What are your Credit Scores?

| | TransUnion | EQUIFAX |
|---|---|---|
| **300-579** (Very Poor) | | |
| **580-639** (Poor) | | |
| **640-699** (Fair) | | |
| **700-749** (Good) | | |
| **750-850** (Excellent) | | |

## Credit Factors

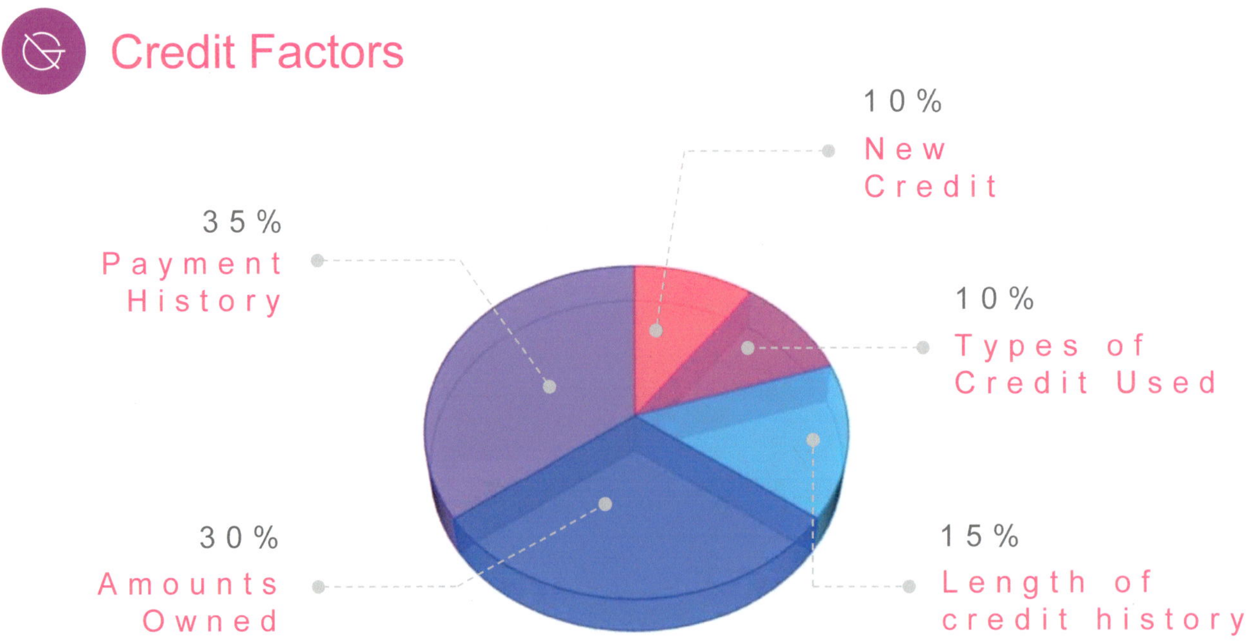


Diagram C shows the factors that personally impact your credit score

# Notes

Diagram C

| Credit card use | Payment history | Derogatory marks |
|---|---|---|
| High Impact | High Impact | High Impact |
| **2%** | **97%** | **2** |
| How much credit you're using compared to your total limits | Percentage of payment you made on time | Collections, tax lines bankruptcies or civil judgments on your report |
| View detail | View detail | View detail |

| Credit age | Total acounts | Hard inquiries |
|---|---|---|
| Medium Impact | Low Impact | Low Impact |
| **4** YRS **9** MOS | **19** | **3** |
| Average age of your open accounts | Total open and closed accounts | Number of times you've applied or credit |
| View detail | View detail | View detail |

As mentioned in *"Keeping Score – What You Need To Know To make Your Credit Score Grow"*, your credit score can vary based on what bureau the creditor decides to report to

# Notes

# Let's see where you stand

TransUnion

| | | | |
|---|---|---|---|
| Credit Card Use | | Credit Age | |
| Payment History | | Total Accounts | |
| Derogatory Marks | | Hard Inquiries | |

EQUIFAX

| | | | |
|---|---|---|---|
| Credit Card Use | | Credit Age | |
| Payment History | | Total Accounts | |
| Derogatory Marks | | Hard Inquiries | |

# Credit Card Use

To optimize your credit score, it is best to keep your balances at 30% of the limit or below. It's not always best to pay off your balances. However, if you have no goals of purchasing a home or car within the next few months and you do not wish to keep a balance on your cards, pay them to zero. But do **NOT** close them

# Notes

# Applying for new credit cards

Credit card payment history is one of the most important things to affect your score outside of late payments. They can absolutely devastate your score, or they can propel you to the elite 800 club. If you do not have a credit card, it is nearly impossible to achieve such credit scores. I get it, some people lack the self-control & discipline to maintain low credit card balances. But if your goal is truly to increase your scores significantly, you must have at least one credit card (multiple are preferred).

The beautiful thing about Credit Karma is they take the guess work out of trying to figure out if a credit card company will approve you or not. They look at your profile, and based upon this, they provide offerings of credit card companies that are likely to approve you for a credit card.

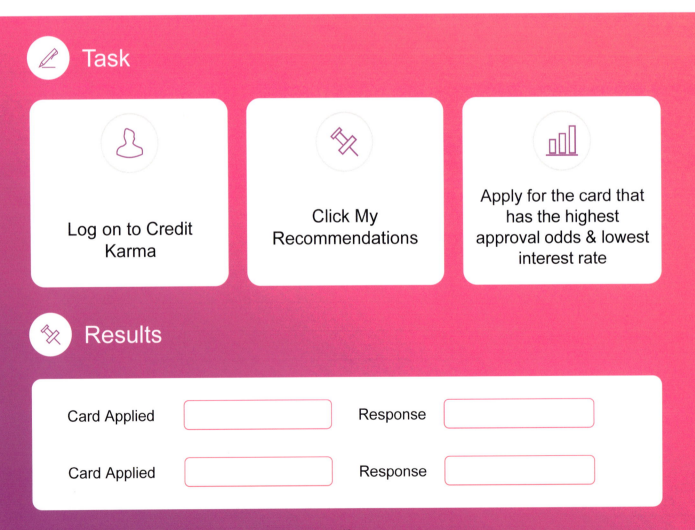

## Task

- Log on to Credit Karma
- Click My Recommendations
- Apply for the card that has the highest approval odds & lowest interest rate

## Results

| Card Applied | | Response | |
|---|---|---|---|
| Card Applied | | Response | |

# Notes

# Optimizing Your Current Credit Cards

01

**Credit Card Name**

| Your Limit | Your Balance | Target Balance |
|---|---|---|
| ________ | ________ | ________ |
| | | = Your Limit times 30% e.g. ($1000 limit x 30% = $300) |

02

**Credit Card Name**

| Your Limit | Your Balance | Target Balance |
|---|---|---|
| ________ | ________ | ________ |
| | | = Your Limit times 30% e.g. ($1000 limit x 30% = $300) |

03

**Credit Card Name**

| Your Limit | Your Balance | Target Balance |
|---|---|---|
| ________ | ________ | ________ |
| | | = Your Limit times 30% e.g. ($1000 limit x 30% = $300) |

# Optimizing Your Current Credit Cards

04

Credit Card Name

| Your Limit | Your Balance | Target Balance |
|---|---|---|
| ______ | ______ | ______ |
| | | = Your Limit times 30% e.g. ($1000 limit x 30% = $300) |

05

Credit Card Name

| Your Limit | Your Balance | Target Balance |
|---|---|---|
| ______ | ______ | ______ |
| | | = Your Limit times 30% e.g. ($1000 limit x 30% = $300) |

06

Credit Card Name

| Your Limit | Your Balance | Target Balance |
|---|---|---|
| ______ | ______ | ______ |
| | | = Your Limit times 30% e.g. ($1000 limit x 30% = $300) |

# Optimizing Your Current Credit Cards

07

## Credit Card Name

| Your Limit | Your Balance | Target Balance |
| --- | --- | --- |
| ______ | ______ | ______ |
| | | = Your Limit times 30% e.g. ($1000 limit x 30% = $300) |

08

## Credit Card Name

| Your Limit | Your Balance | Target Balance |
| --- | --- | --- |
| ______ | ______ | ______ |
| | | = Your Limit times 30% e.g. ($1000 limit x 30% = $300) |

09

## Credit Card Name

| Your Limit | Your Balance | Target Balance |
| --- | --- | --- |
| ______ | ______ | ______ |
| | | = Your Limit times 30% e.g. ($1000 limit x 30% = $300) |

# 10 Optimizing Your Current Credit Cards

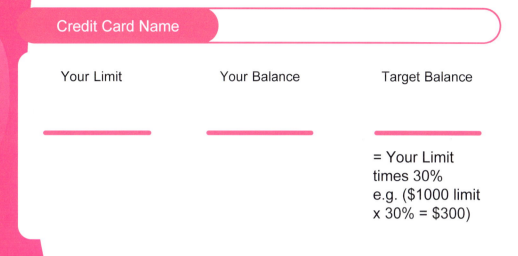

**Credit Card Name**

| Your Limit | Your Balance | Target Balance |
|---|---|---|
| ______ | ______ | ______ |
| | | = Your Limit times 30% e.g. ($1000 limit x 30% = $300) |

## What were the results of lowering your credit card utilization?

Total Credit Score increase

## Limit Increase

Paying your credit card down to 30% of the limit may not be feasible for you to do within a short timeframe.

If you have good payment history, your credit card company may grant you a credit limit increase.

Contact your credit card company (this can be done online on their portal) and request a limit increase. This *may* create an inquiry on your credit report depending on the company. Contact them to confirm before doing so. Keep in mind, inquiries are only 10%, but revolving debt balance is 30% of your credit score. It may be worth getting the inquiry if it will reduce your utilization.

# Paying down your credit cards to 30%

What were the results?

# Shopping Cart Trick

The shopping cart trick, also known as the soft pull trick, is a clever method that allows people with bad credit to get a credit card. The shopping cart trick relies on the fact that many websites will pre-approve you for a credit card during the checkout process without actually checking your score. This means you can get a card without a "hard pull" as well as still get a card with bad credit.

- You need to be opted in for credit card promotional emails. You're automatically opted in, so unless you have manually opted out you won't need to do anything.
- Only works on cards issued by Comenity Bank (and some cards issued by Synchrony & Wells Fargo)
- Turn your pop up blocker off if you use one. A lot of the credit card offers pop up, if you have a pop up blocker then you might miss it.
- If you're asked for your full SSN, it might be a hard pull. Some of these websites ask for your full SSN when applying for the store cards, while others ask for your last four digits. If it asks for your full SSN it might be a hard pull so be careful.
- Go to the website of the store you want a card for.
- Join their loyalty program (some people find more success skipping this step and just checking out as a guest)
- Add some items to your shopping cart
- Start to check out
- Enter in your address, make sure this matches your address listed in your credit reports exactly
- Continue going through the checkout process until you get to the final payment page. You should receive your offer before this page, if you haven't then either the shopping cart trick isn't working or you need to try again.
- Choose to accept your offer
- Complete the application

You don't need to actually purchase anything at the store you use this trick on. Once your application is finished you'll automatically be taken back to your check out page (if this was closed earlier) you can just abandon this after you've finished applying.

This is not a guarantee, but 90% of the clients that I recommended try this were approved. If you aren't approved, you have nothing to lose but a few minutes of your time, as you will likely not have a hard credit pull on your file.

Bank Store Credit Cards that will likely work

| | | | | |
|---|---|---|---|---|
| Abercrombie & Fitch | Ann Taylor | Bath & Body Works | Brylane Home | Buckle |
| Coldwater Creek | Express | Gamestop | HSN | J. Crew |
| Jessica London | JJill | King Size Direct | Loft | Motorola |
| MyPoints | New York & Co. | One Stop Plus | Overstock | PacSun |
| Romans | Sportsman Guide | Total Rewards | Venus | Victoria Secrets |
| Wayfair | Williams Sonoma | Woman Within | Synchrony (QVC & Walmart) | Wells Fargo (Dillards & Kirkland) |

## Shopping Cart Trick

Card Applied ________ Response ________

Card Applied ________ Response ________

# Notes

# Balance Transfer

Balance transfers are great ways to boost your score by simply transferring the balance from one credit card to another. Only do this if it is going to reduce your utilization on all cards to 30% of the limit. If it is not reducing your utilization to 30%, the only other reason it makes sense is if you are trying to save money on interest, and the balance transfer is helping you to pay off the credit card quicker.

## How to transfer balance

Contact customer service (the number should be on the back of your card)

Log on to your online account and follow the instructions on how to do a balance transfer

# Notes

# Authorized User

An authorized user account is one of the quickest ways you can boost your score without any personal input or responsibility. Becoming an authorized user happens when you are added on to someone else's credit card account. You have authority to use it (if they provide you with the credit card), but more importantly, you are given all of the primary users credit history. Good, bad, beautiful, or ugly. For this purpose, it is extremely important that you are only added on to a beautiful card. Here are the rules to maximizing your score with an authorized user account.

- You trust the primary account holder
- They've had the card for a lengthy period of time (2+ years is best)
- They keep low balances, preferably under 30% of the limit
- They do not have or plan to have any 30-day late payments
- They do not go above or never have been above the credit card limit.

# How to get added to an Authorized User Account

01 The account holder can contact the credit card company by phone and add you on

02 The account holder can log on to their account online and select Add Authorized user.

If this credit card is hurting your score, you should remove it from your credit profile immediately. You can do so by:

01 Contacting the credit card company over the phone and requesting that you be removed from the account (easiest way)

02 Send a letter in writing requesting your removal

| | |
|---|---|
| Account Holder | |
| Date Added | |
| Credit Score Results | |

# Removing Late Payments from your credit report

Sometimes creditors are willing to remove 30 day late payments from your credit report. You simply call and ask for a Courtesy Late Removal. It's a 50/50 chance but certainly worth a shot. If they agree to do this, ask them to send you something in writing, preferably by fax or email. Diagram F is an example of a courtesy late removal.

# Notes

# Courtesy Late Removal from Credit Card Company

Diagram F

Macy's
P.O. Box 8228
Mason, OH 45040

In Response To Your Request

Account Ending [redacted]
www.macys.com/mymacyscard

XE00196446 1 AT 0.399 Z5149942 TMN 032867 0610

Month late removed

November 17, 2011

**Why we're writing you**
Thank you for your recent request to have your Macy's Credit Card Account, [redacted] corrected on your credit report. We have reviewed your request and have notified the consumer reporting agencies listed below to delete the following derogatory information:

- 02/2016

Equifax Credit Information Service
P.O. Box 740241
Atlanta, GA 30374-0241
1-800-685-1111
www.equifax.com

TransUnion LLC
Consumer Relations Center
P.O. Box 1000
Chester, PA 19022
1-800-888-4213
www.transunion.com

Experian
P.O. Box 2002
Allen, TX 75013-0036
1-888 EXPERIAN (1-888-397-3742)
www.experian.com

Please allow at least 30 days for the consumer reporting agencies to update their files.

**How to contact us**
If you have additional questions, our Representatives are available to assist you. Please contact us online at www.macys.com/mymacyscard, or at the phone number below.

Thank you for giving us the opportunity to be of service to you. We look forward to serving you again in the future.

Sincerely,

Consumer Credit Specialist Dept
Phone: 1-800-243-6552
TDD/TTY – Hearing or Speech Impaired: 1-800-281-0820

**FEDERAL REGULATIONS REQUIRE THE STATEMENT PRINTED ON THE REVERSE SIDE**
**Thank You**

# Notes

# AnnualCreditReport.com

Let's go over to AnnualCreditReport.com to see how to read their credit report

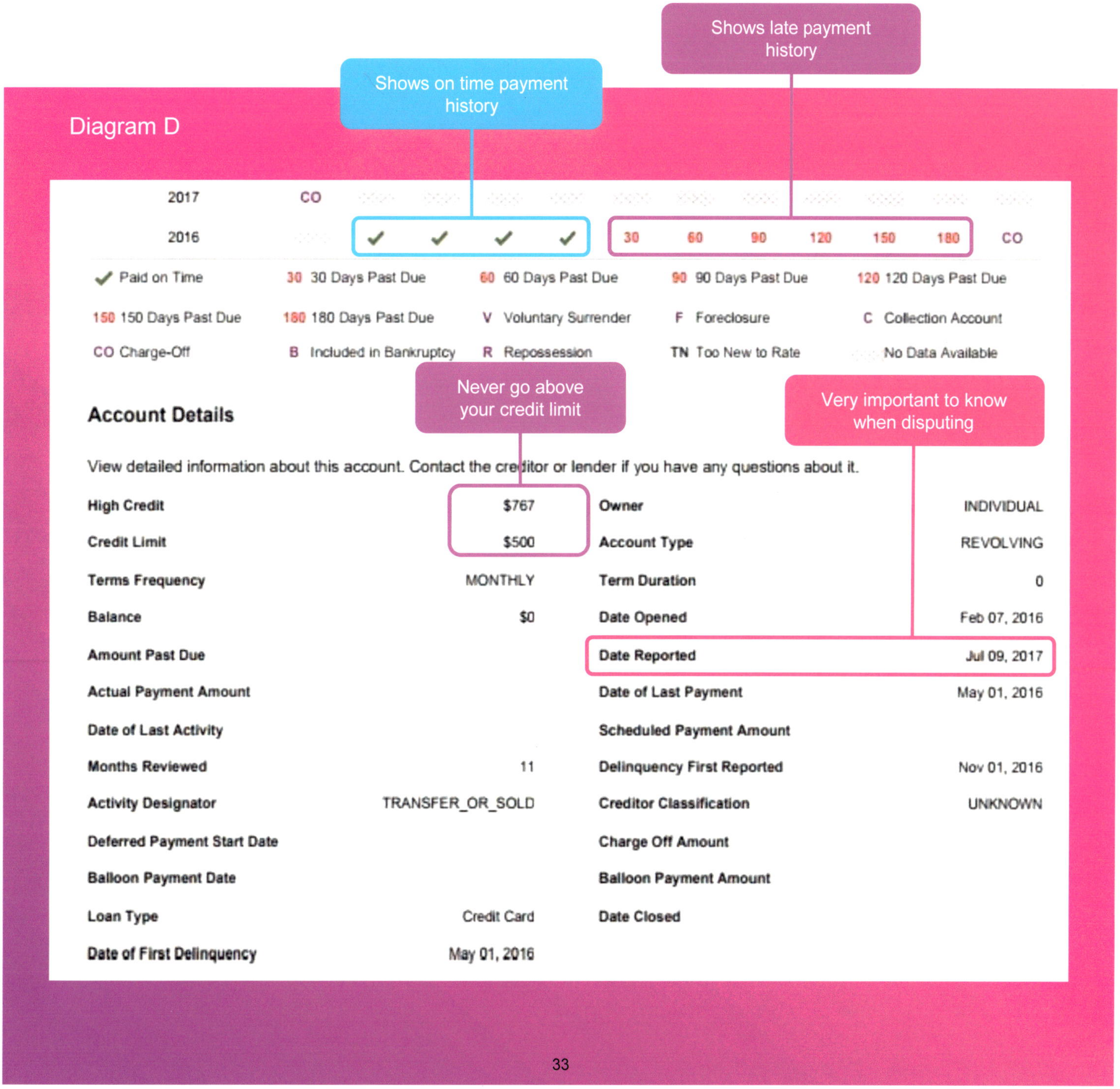

Shows late payment history

Shows on time payment history

Diagram D

| | | | | | | | | | | | | |
|---|---|---|---|---|---|---|---|---|---|---|---|---|
| 2017 | CO | | | | | | | | | | | |
| 2016 | | ✓ | ✓ | ✓ | ✓ | 30 | 60 | 90 | 120 | 150 | 180 | CO |

✓ Paid on Time | 30 30 Days Past Due | 60 60 Days Past Due | 90 90 Days Past Due | 120 120 Days Past Due

150 150 Days Past Due | 180 180 Days Past Due | V Voluntary Surrender | F Foreclosure | C Collection Account

CO Charge-Off | B Included in Bankruptcy | R Repossession | TN Too New to Rate | No Data Available

Never go above your credit limit

Very important to know when disputing

## Account Details

View detailed information about this account. Contact the creditor or lender if you have any questions about it.

| | | | |
|---|---|---|---|
| **High Credit** | $767 | **Owner** | INDIVIDUAL |
| **Credit Limit** | $500 | **Account Type** | REVOLVING |
| **Terms Frequency** | MONTHLY | **Term Duration** | 0 |
| **Balance** | $0 | **Date Opened** | Feb 07, 2016 |
| **Amount Past Due** | | **Date Reported** | Jul 09, 2017 |
| **Actual Payment Amount** | | **Date of Last Payment** | May 01, 2016 |
| **Date of Last Activity** | | **Scheduled Payment Amount** | |
| **Months Reviewed** | 11 | **Delinquency First Reported** | Nov 01, 2016 |
| **Activity Designator** | TRANSFER_OR_SOLD | **Creditor Classification** | UNKNOWN |
| **Deferred Payment Start Date** | | **Charge Off Amount** | |
| **Balloon Payment Date** | | **Balloon Payment Amount** | |
| **Loan Type** | Credit Card | **Date Closed** | |
| **Date of First Delinquency** | May 01, 2016 | | |

# Credit Negotiations

It is important to understand which accounts you should be concerned with. While all accounts affect your credit score, collection accounts that haven't reported in over 2 years won't affect your scores as much as a more recently reported account. Disputing the wrong account can "wake up the dead" and drop your score.

On AnnualCreditReport.com (below) there is a section on the credit report that shows you the last date the account was reported.

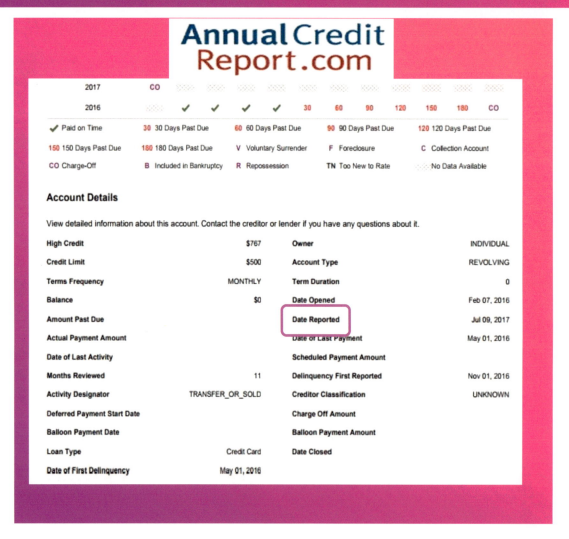

**Annual Credit Report.com**

| | | | | | | | | | | | | |
|---|---|---|---|---|---|---|---|---|---|---|---|---|
| 2017 | CO | | | | | | | | | | | |
| 2016 | | ✓ | ✓ | ✓ | ✓ | 30 | 60 | 90 | 120 | 150 | 180 | CO |

| | | | | |
|---|---|---|---|---|
| ✓ Paid on Time | 30 30 Days Past Due | 60 60 Days Past Due | 90 90 Days Past Due | 120 120 Days Past Due |
| 150 150 Days Past Due | 180 180 Days Past Due | V Voluntary Surrender | F Foreclosure | C Collection Account |
| CO Charge-Off | B Included in Bankruptcy | R Repossession | TN Too New to Rate | No Data Available |

**Account Details**

View detailed information about this account. Contact the creditor or lender if you have any questions about it.

| | | | |
|---|---|---|---|
| **High Credit** | $767 | **Owner** | INDIVIDUAL |
| **Credit Limit** | $500 | **Account Type** | REVOLVING |
| **Terms Frequency** | MONTHLY | **Term Duration** | 0 |
| **Balance** | $0 | **Date Opened** | Feb 07, 2016 |
| **Amount Past Due** | | **Date Reported** | Jul 09, 2017 |
| **Actual Payment Amount** | | **Date of Last Payment** | May 01, 2016 |
| **Date of Last Activity** | | **Scheduled Payment Amount** | |
| **Months Reviewed** | 11 | **Delinquency First Reported** | Nov 01, 2016 |
| **Activity Designator** | TRANSFER_OR_SOLD | **Creditor Classification** | UNKNOWN |
| **Deferred Payment Start Date** | | **Charge Off Amount** | |
| **Balloon Payment Date** | | **Balloon Payment Amount** | |
| **Loan Type** | Credit Card | **Date Closed** | |
| **Date of First Delinquency** | May 01, 2016 | | |

## Debt Settlement

It's wonderful if you want to be fiscally responsible and pay all collections on your credit report. It's not a bad idea, however, paying or settling the debt will likely not increase your credit score. In fact, it may drop your score if the collection has not been reported in 2 years. The status will change from a collection to a *paid* collection with a current reported date.

If you still wish to pay or settle your debt, I recommend settling for the following reasons:

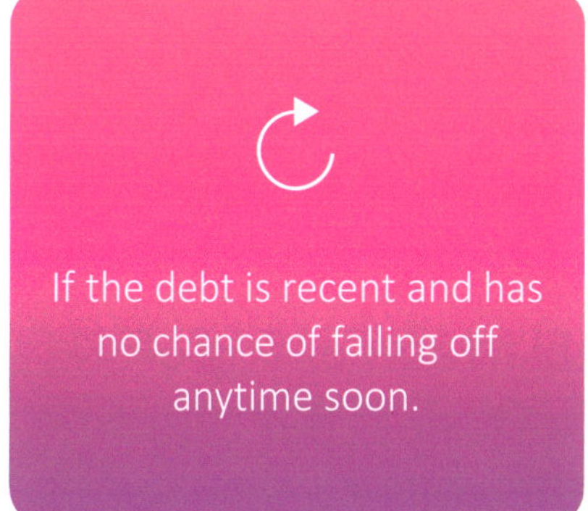

If the debt is recent and has no chance of falling off anytime soon.

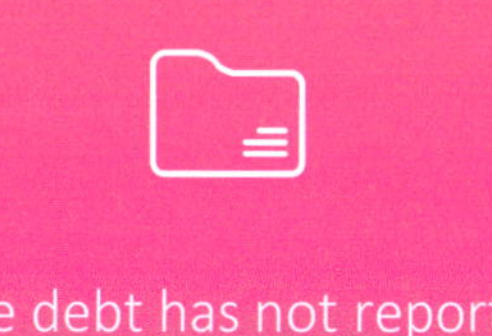

If the debt has not reported in over 2 years, but you don't mind taking a hit on your credit score.

If it is a requirement to secure home loan financing (seek guidance from your lender before settling)

## Task

Contact the collection agency and make an offer. Start low by offering to pay 30 percent or less of what you owe and negotiate your way to an amount that you and the collector can both agree upon. Make your offer attractive, and make sure that it's something that you can actually stick with. If you are unable to pay the debt in full, request payment arrangements. This can be done either over the phone or in writing

# Debt Settlement Letter

Name & Address

Collector's Name & Address

Date

Re: Account Number XXXX-XXXX-XXXX-XXXX

This letter is in response to your call/letter/credit report entry on (date) for the account referenced above. I would like to pay off or settle this debt in full and save both of our time and efforts.

I'd like to clarify that I am not acknowledging or accepting that I owe this debt. I respectfully request that you properly verify your right to collect on this debt, in addition to providing me with an accounting of the amount I owe. I am aware that your company can report the debt to the credit bureaus as necessary and that you have the ability to change the account status since you are the information provider.

I hope you'll also agree to not discuss this offer with any third party (except the original creditor). If you find my offer acceptable, please send me a letter agreeing to these terms, signed by your authorized representative, and subject to the laws of my state.

Under the Fair Debt Collection Practices Act, I have the right to dispute this alleged debt. If I do not receive your postmarked response within the next 15 business days, I shall withdraw my offer.

Please forward your agreement to my address listed above.

Sincerely,

# Debt Settlement Results

Contacted the following Creditors:

Name | Date Contacted

Response

Name | Date Contacted

Response

Name | Date Contacted

Response

Name | Date Contacted

Response

Name | Date Contacted

Response

# Notes

# Disputing errors on your credit report

All 3 credit bureaus have a legal obligation to comply with the Federal Credit Reporting Act. They are only allowed to report negative items if they are 100% accurate and verifiable. By saying accurate, it means that all of the information is correct. 1) The amount owed 2) Date opened 3)Account number. Since 1 in 3 Americans have errors on their credit report, chances are, you have negative items that you can dispute and get removed. The burden of proof is on the credit bureaus, not you as the consumer. However, when you dispute online, you are signing an arbitration clause that states that they do not have to verify the items (among other things). That is why its always important to dispute negative accounts in writing.

Over the next several pages, we will discuss 3 rounds of disputes to remove erroneous items from your credit file.

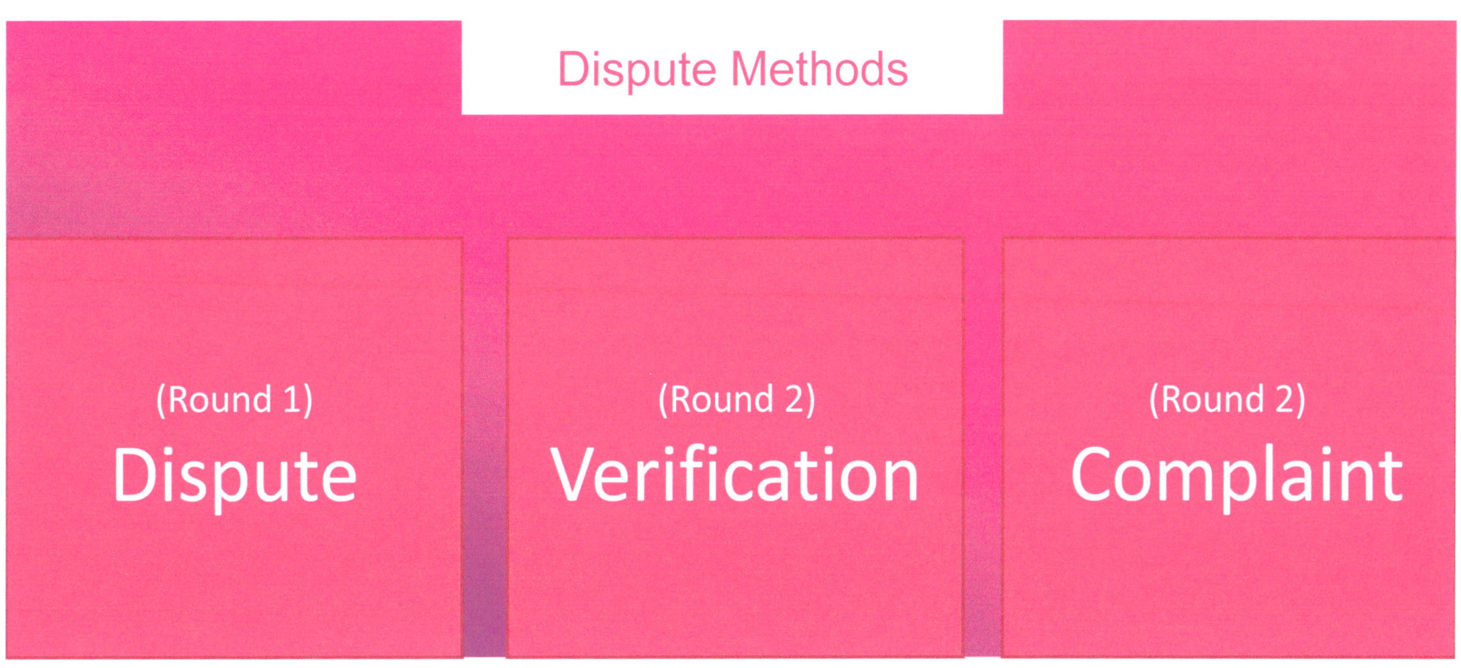

Round 1

# Disputes: Removing negative items on your credit

All disputes should be in writing and you should only send your dispute to the bureau that is reporting the debt. Credit Karma & AnnualCreditReport.com both provide separate reports and you can verify where your creditor is reporting.

## Credit Bureaus

| Experian | Equifax | Transunion |
|---|---|---|
| 701 Experian Pkwy | PO BOX 740241 | 2 Baldwin Pl |
| P.O. Box 2002 | Atlanta, GA | PO Box 1000 |
| Allen, TX 75013 | 30374-0241 | Chester, PA 19022 |
| www.experian.com | www.equifax.com | www.transunion.com |
| 888-397-3742 | 800-685-1111 | 800-888-4213 |

## Common errors include

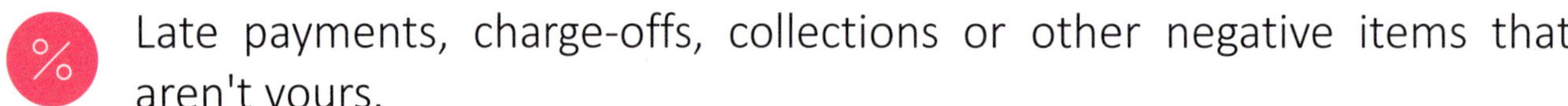

Late payments, charge-offs, collections or other negative items that aren't yours.

Credit limits reported as lower than they really are.

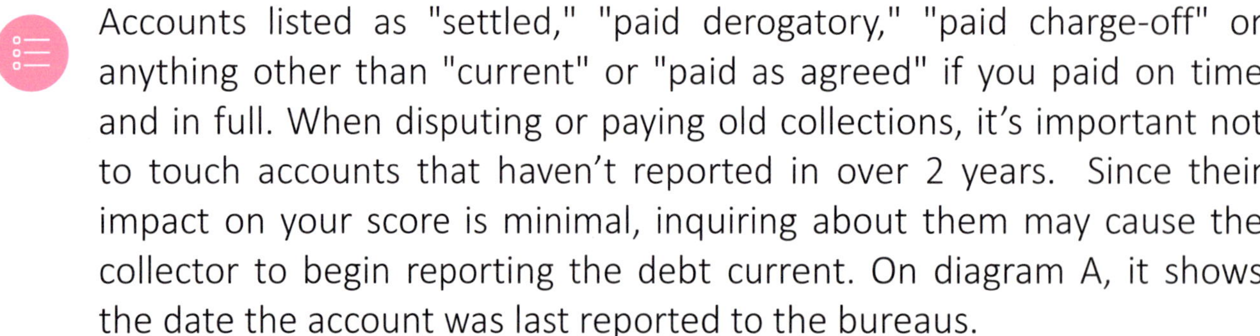

Accounts listed as "settled," "paid derogatory," "paid charge-off" or anything other than "current" or "paid as agreed" if you paid on time and in full. When disputing or paying old collections, it's important not to touch accounts that haven't reported in over 2 years. Since their impact on your score is minimal, inquiring about them may cause the collector to begin reporting the debt current. On diagram A, it shows the date the account was last reported to the bureaus.

## Round 1

# Dispute Letter

Your Name & Address

Collector's Name & Address

Date

Re: Account Number XXXX-XXXX-XXXX-XXXX

Re: Correction of erroneous/inaccurate information in my consumer credit file/report.

Dear (Credit Bureau):
I just recently received a copy of my credit report and noticed a number of outdated and incorrect information in my file. Please begin an immediate investigation of the following items listed below in my credit report. Please address the following items immediately and send me an updated corrected copy of my report at the conclusion of your investigation.

1. Account disputes
a. Aurora Bank FSB Acct xxxx – this was not a foreclosure, this was included in my bankruptcy
b. Bank of America Acct#xxx – This is not my account
c. Homeward Residential #xxxx– This is not my account
2. The following AKA/Alias information should be deleted from my credit profile as they are not valid/accurate
a. Name Aliases that should be removed
3. The following addresses should be deleted from my credit profile as they are not valid/accurate
a. List all addresses other than your current that appears on your credit report
Thank you for your help and prompt attention to this matter
Your Name & Signature

# 3 Things to remember when disputing

It's important to know that credit bureaus do not work with 3rd party companies offering credit repair service. The way they ensure that you are the correct party disputing your personal information is by you providing the following items:

**1**
A copy of your Driver License or Identification

**2**
A copy of your Social Security Card

**3**
Your Signature on the dispute letter

Credit bureaus have 30 days to contact the creditor to verify if the debt is yours. If the creditor does not respond, the bureau must remove it from your credit report. But if they do respond, the bureau will continue reporting. Important note: If you dispute an item that hasn't reported in 2 years (see diagram D), you risk the chance of the company reporting this collection current and it can drop your score.

# Notes

## Round 2

# Disputes: Method of Verification

After you have completed your disputes, the credit bureaus have 30 days to provide a response in writing. Sometimes they will remove the negative accounts, other times, they will "verify" they are indeed your debts. The problem with this is most of the time, they haven't actually completed proper verification. Per FCRA, common bureau violations include:

- Not notifying a creditor that you dispute the debt that it has reported
- Not conducting a reasonable investigation of your dispute, or
- Not correcting or deleting any inaccurate, incomplete or unverifiable information within 30 days of the receiving notice of your dispute.

You as the consumer have the right to request a <u>Method of Verification Proof</u>. Since credit bureaus receive upwards of 10,000 disputes a month, the most efficient way for them to verify disputes is by automation. This dispute requires a manual investigation. Only do this method after you have completed your first round. Send this to the bureau that did **not** provide you the desired response. Do not send to the bureau that deleted the account from your credit file You are now requesting to know:
1)Who they spoke with
2)The number they called
3)How long they spoke to them
4)The credit bureau's rep that made the phone call
5)The docs used to verify this debt was yours

This dispute should be sent by **<u>Certified Mail</u>** so that it can be used in round 3 if necessary. The burden of proof is on the credit bureaus and not on you as the consumer, so be vigilant about receiving the proper information on your credit report. Normally completing this step is enough, but if not, Round 3 may do the trick.

Round 2

# Method of Verification Letter

Date:
Credit Bureau Name & Address
Your Name, Address Social & DOB
Re: Request to provide method of verification

To Whom It May Concern: On [Insert Original Dispute Date],

I requested an investigation because I felt the item is not being reported legally, and on [Insert Date of Response] I received a letter stating that your investigation was complete. Please answer the following questions: What certified documents were reviewed to conclude your investigation? Please provide me a complete copy of all of the information that was transmitted to the data furnisher as part of the investigation, as required by FCRA:

- Who did you speak with?
- What was the date?
- How long was the conversation?
- What was their position?
- What number did you call?
- What is the name of your employee that spoke directly to the creditor?
- What is the position of your employee that spoke to the creditor?

This inaccurate reporting has caused me severe financial and emotional distress. Please reply within 15 days to the above questions, or delete the items.
Sincerely,

Your name

# Notes

Round 3

# Disputes: Letter of Complaint with the FTC

Although you've given the credit bureaus 15 days to respond, wait about 30 days to hear back. Round two generally should do the trick, however, if you do not receive the desired response, or they simply ignore your request, send this 3rd and final **Certified letter** to the bureaus threatening to file a complaint with the Federal Trade Commission. The FTC is an independent federal agency whose main goals are to protect the consumers. If the credit bureaus are not accurately reporting, they can be fined by the FTC.

As with everything, patience is paramount.

Round 3

# Letter of Complaint to FTC

Date:
Credit Bureau Name & Address
Your Name, Address Social & DOB
RE: Follow-up Dispute Letter of (insert date of original validation request letter)

**NOTICE OF INTENT TO FILE COMPLAINT**

To Whom It May Concern:
This letter shall serve as formal notice of my intent to file a complaint with the FTC, due to your disregard of the law. You claim to have somehow verified the items I requested. Therefore, I legally requested a description of the procedures used to verify the information. As indicated by the attached copy of the letter and mailing receipt [Insert Date on Receipt], you received and accepted through registered mail my request letter dated [Insert Date of Your Letter]. To date you have not responded to this request and have thus not performed your duty mentioned in the law. Federal law requires you to respond within 15 days, yet you have failed to respond and it has been over 30 days. Failure to comply with these federal regulations by credit reporting agencies is investigated by the Federal Trade Commission (see 15 USC 41, et seq.). I am maintaining a careful record of my communications with you on this matter; for the purpose of filing a complaint with the FTC, unless I hear from you in 20 days. For the record, the following information is being erroneously included on my credit report. [List all company name( s) and account number( s)] You claimed to have verified the erroneous information, yet you refuse to tell me HOW you were able to verify these accounts. If you do not immediately remove this inaccurate and/ or incomplete information, I will file a formal complaint with the FTC. As I stated, I am carefully documenting these events, including the lack of response REQUIRED under federal law from you. Any further delay is inexcusable.

Sincerely,

Your Name

# Notes

# Inquires & Personal information on your report

Credit inquiries are requests by a 'legitimate business' to check your credit. As far as your credit score is concerned, credit inquiries are classified as either 'hard inquiries' or 'soft inquiries' – only hard inquiries have a negative effect on your credit score. Depending on the types of loans you are applying for, you can apply with multiple lending institutions without multiple inquiries negatively impacting you. For example, if you were applying for a home or car loan, it is understandable that your credit may be run several times. As long as it is done within a 30-day window, it will have minimal impact on your credit score.

A little known fact is that if you have too many variables with your name aliases, multiple addresses, PO Box, and multiple jobs listed on your credit, it will negatively affect your credit score. This section of the credit report, you can clean it up and dispute all of the items that are not current.

# Disputing inquiries from your credit report

Although inquiries are only 10% of your credit score, it can reduce your score significantly if you have too many. Send this letter to the 3 credit bureaus to have erroneous inquiries investigated and removed

Credit Bureau Name & Address

Your Name, Address Social & DOB

Re: Removal of erroneous inquiries from my credit file

Dear (Credit Bureau):

I reviewed a copy of my credit report and (Company Name) ran an unauthorized credit inquiry (Date)

I never authorized such action and this constitutes a violation of my rights under the Fair Credit Reporting Act §604 as well as a violation of my rights to privacy.  Please investigate this occurrence and respond back in writing immediately.

If you have any questions or need additional information, please contact me at address listed above.

Thank you,

Signature

# Disputing aliases & personal info from your credit report

Simply cleaning up aliases and removing old addresses from credit reports can increase your credit score. To do this, send a dispute letter to the 3 credit bureaus. This should also be accompanied by a copy of your current Driver License & Social Security Card to confirm your correct information.

The letter should say the following:

Date:

Credit Bureau Name & Address

Your Name, Address Social & DOB

Re: Correction of erroneous/inaccurate information in my consumer credit file/report.

Dear (Credit Bureau):

I just recently received a copy of my credit report and noticed outdated and incorrect personal information in my file. Please see my license that I have attached and update my credit file to only reflect my name, **Joan Mary Doe**, my birthday **July 3, 1991**, and my current address **4225 Main Street Anywhere, CA 90048**. Please provide a copy of my report with the updated information as soon as possible

Thank you,

Signature

# Removing Aliases

| | |
|---|---|
| Date Submitted | |
| Results | |
| Credit Score Results | |

# Disputes

What were the results?

#  Pay for Deletion Phone Call

Pay for deletion is a strategy used to have items removed from your credit report. Do NOT confuse this with a settlement or pay to zero balance. Creditors will often advise you that paying a collection balance to zero will have the same effects on your credit score. It **WILL NOT!** Paying a collection to zero will simply be a paid collection that will hurt your score equal to a collection with an outstanding balance. When negotiating a deletion, you can start your negotiations with a lower payment offer, however, creditors are more likely to work with you if you pay the debt in full. When you speak to the representative, advise them that you are willing to pay (amount) **only** if they are willing to delete the item from your credit report. If they agree to delete, advise that before you make payment, you want something in writing to attest to the fact that they will delete the debt and you will pay within the timeframe that you discussed. They typically want you to pay the full amount within a 24-hour period. If you are serious about getting your items removed, be prepared to pay the item in full immediately.

I have been successful at getting this done without the creditor sending something in writing. Sometimes they do not have the ability to verify in writing prior to payment receipt. Most reputable collection agencies record all calls. It's also not a bad idea for you to record the call and document all verifying information from the representative if they cannot provide you a document in writing. On the following page, you will see an example of a deletion letter from a collection agency. Simply provide a copy of the letter along with a dispute letter **to the reporting credit bureau** and they will remove it from your credit file

# Deletion letter from collection agency

Diagram E

November 30, 2016

SAN JOSE, CA 95136-4505

Collection account for: VALLEY RAD SAM WOMEN'S CENTER
C.C.C. account number:
PIN:

Dear .

The above referenced collection account has been satisfied and is now closed with this office. The item will be deleted from the records of Experian, Trans Union and Equifax and should not be considered a hindrance to obtaining credit.

Sincerely,

Maria Fioni Ext 2585

This communication is from a debt collector.

# Pay for Deletion Letter in Writing

Your Name & Address

Collector's Name & Address

Date

Re: Account Number XXXX-XXXX-XXXX-XXXX

Dear Collection Manager:

This letter is in response to your **(letter / call / credit report entry)** on **(date)** related to the debt referenced above. I wish to save us both some time and effort by settling this debt.

Please be aware that this is not an acknowledgment or acceptance of the debt, as I have not received any verification of the debt. Nor is this a promise to pay and is not a payment agreement unless you provide a response as detailed below.

I am aware that your company can report this debt to the credit bureaus as you deem necessary.

Furthermore, you can change the listing since you are the information furnisher.

I am willing to pay (this debt in full / $XXX as settlement for this debt) in return for your agreement to remove all information regarding this debt from the credit reporting agencies within ten calendar days of payment.

If you agree to the terms, I will send certified payment in the amount of $XXX payable to (Collection Agency) in exchange to have all information related to this debt removed from all of my credit files.

If you accept this offer, you also agree not to discuss the offer with any third-party, excluding the original creditor. If you accept the offer, please prepare a letter on your company letterhead agreeing to the terms. This letter should be signed by an authorized agent of (Collection Agency). The letter will be treated as a contract and subject to the laws of my state.

As granted by the Fair Debt Collection Practices Act, I have the right to dispute this alleged debt. If I do not receive your postmarked response within 15 days, I will withdraw the offer and request full verification of this debt.

Please forward your agreement to the address listed above.

Sincerely,

# Pay for Deletion

Contacted the following Creditors:

Name | Date Contacted

Response

Name | Date Contacted

Response

# Notes

# Debt Validation

Must validate

As a consumer, the most powerful weapon you have for fighting collections that appear on your report is requiring that the collection agency validate the debt. By law, you have the right to request they validate any and all debt they are trying to collect. This goes a step further from just disputing items on your credit report. If they cannot provide validation in writing, they are required to remove the item from your report and cease contacting you immediately.

The following are items you can ask them to validate:

01

Agreement with the creditor that authorizes you to collect on this alleged debt

02

The agreement bearing my signature stating that I have agreed to assume the debt

03

Valid copies of the debt agreement stating the amount of the debt and interest charges

04

Proof that the Statute of Limitations has not expired

05

Complete payment history on this account along with an accounting of all additional charges being assessed

06

You are licensed to collect in my state; and your license numbers and Registered Agent

# Debt Validation

In accordance with the Fair Debt Collection Practices Act (FDCPA), you can challenge the validity of a debt. On the following page there is a sample debt validation letter that you can use to request the creditor/collection agency verify that the debt is yours and you are legally bound to it.

**If you have collections on your credit report and you do not believe they are valid, download this letter and send it directly to the creditors**. The best method is by Certified Mail. This way you can confirm they received the letter, and if you need to file a complaint to the CFPB for no response, you have proof of service.

If you have not heard from the creditor within the legal time given, file a complaint with the CFPB, and the collection agency can be fined

- File online at www.consumerfinance.gov/Complaint
- Call the toll-free phone number at 1-855-411-CFPB (2372) or TTY/TDD phone number at 1-855-729-CFPB (2372)
- Fax the CFPB at 1-855-237-2392
- Mail a letter to: Consumer Financial Protection Bureau, P.O. Box 4503, Iowa City, Iowa 52244

# Debt Validation Letter

Date:

Name: & Address:

Phone:

Collection Agency: & Address:

Acct#:

I am writing this letter in response to the phone call/letter received from you on (Date). In conformance to my rights under the Fair Debt Collection Practices Act (FDCPA), I am requesting you to provide me with a validation of the debt that you talked of earlier. Please note, this a not a refusal to pay, rather a statement that your claim is disputed and validation is demanded. (15 USC 1692g Sec. 809 (b))

I do hereby request that your office provide me with complete documentation to verify that I owe the said debt and have any legal obligation to pay you.

Please provide me with the following:

1. Agreement with the creditor that authorizes you to collect on this alleged debt
2. The agreement bearing my signature stating that I have agreed to assume the debt
3. Valid copies of the debt agreement stating the amount of the debt and interest charges
4. Proof that the Statute of Limitations has not expired
5. Complete payment history on this account along with an accounting of all additional charges being assessed
6. Show me that you are licensed to collect in my state; and your license numbers and Registered Agent

If your office fails to reply to this debt validation letter within 30 days from the date of your receipt, all instances related to this account must be immediately deleted and completely removed from my credit file. Moreover, all future attempts to collect on the said debt must be ceased.

Your non-compliance with my request will also be construed as an absolute waiver of all claims to enforce the debt against me and your implied agreement to compensate me for court costs and attorney fees if I am forced to bring this matter before a judge.

Thank you,

Your Signature

# Debt Validation Results

Date Submitted:

Collections disputed:

Certified Mail:

Regular Mail:

Response received:

# Failure to Validate Letter

If the collection agency does not respond with ALL of the items listed in your original request send a Failure to Validate letter by Certified Mail.

Date:

Name: & Address:

Phone:

Collection Agency: & Address:

Acct#:

This letter is formal notice that you have failed to provide a complete response to my request for validation received by you on (Date), sent by Certified Mail, postmarked (Date).

The information you provided is incomplete. In your correspondence, you provided on (Date) you stated that in response to my request under the Fair Debt Collection Practices Act, 15 USC 1692g Sec. 809 (B); that you all will continue to resume debt collection. I am writing to request and notify that all attempts must cease and desist immediately as my request has not been responded to in completion. Your offices have failed to respond to or failed to provide **all-inclusive** documentation as specifically requested by the validation request within 30 days from the date of receipt, all references to this account must be deleted and completely removed from my credit files and a copy of the deletion request should be sent to me immediately.

# Notes

# Statute of Limitations on Debt

Under state laws, there are often legal time limits within which a creditor or debt collector must start a lawsuit or the claim may be "barred." These laws are called "statutes of limitation. If you're sued about a debt and the debt is too old, you may have a defense to the lawsuit.

In some states, the statute of limitations period begins when you failed to make a required payment on a debt. In other states it is counted from when you made your most recent payment, even if that payment was made during collection. In some states, even a partial payment on the debt will restart the time-period.

Debts fall into one of four categories. It's important to know which type of debt you have because the time limits are different for each type. Ask an attorney if you have questions about which type of debt you have.

Oral Agreements are debts that were made in an oral contract. With an oral contract, you only made a verbal agreement to pay back the money. Nothing was in writing.

Written Contracts are debts with a contract that was signed by you and the creditor. A contract includes terms and conditions of the loan, e.g. the amount of the loan and monthly payment. A medical debt would be a type of written contract.

Promissory Note is a written agreement to pay back a debt in certain payments, at a certain interest rate and by a certain date and time. Mortgages and student loans are types of promissory notes.

An Open-Ended Account is an account with a revolving balance that you can repay and borrow again. Credit cards, in-store credit, and lines of credit are open-ended accounts. If you can only borrow the money on time, it is not an open-ended account.

# Notes

Below is the time-period for statute of limitations on debt per state.

| State | Oral | Written | Promissory | Open |
|---|---|---|---|---|
| Alabama | 6 | 6 | 6 | 3 |
| Alaska | 6 | 6 | 3 | 3 |
| Arizona | 3 | 6 | 6 | 3 |
| Arkansas | 6 | 6 | 3 | 3 |
| California | 2 | 4 | 4 | 4 |
| Colorado | 6 | 6 | 6 | 6 |
| Connecticut | 3 | 6 | 6 | 3 |
| Delaware | 3 | 3 | 3 | 4 |
| Florida | 4 | 5 | 5 | 4 |
| Georgia | 4 | 6 | 6 | 4 |
| Hawaii | 6 | 6 | 6 | 6 |
| Idaho | 4 | 5 | 5 | 4 |
| Illinois | 5 | 10 | 10 | 5 |
| Indiana | 6 | 10 | 10 | 6 |
| Iowa | 5 | 10 | 5 | 5 |

| State | Oral | Written | Promissory | Open |
|---|---|---|---|---|
| Kansas | 3 | 6 | 5 | 3 |
| Kentucky | 5 | 15 | 15 | 5 |
| Louisiana | 10 | 10 | 10 | 3 |
| Maine | 6 | 6 | 6 | 6 |
| Maryland | 3 | 3 | 6 | 3 |
| Massachusetts | 6 | 6 | 6 | 6 |
| Michigan | 6 | 6 | 6 | 6 |
| Minnesota | 6 | 6 | 6 | 6 |
| Mississippi | 3 | 3 | 3 | 3 |
| Missouri | 5 | 10 | 10 | 5 |
| Montana | 5 | 8 | 8 | 5 |
| Nebraska | 4 | 5 | 5 | 4 |
| Nevada | 4 | 6 | 3 | 4 |
| New Hampshire | 3 | 3 | 6 | 3 |
| New Jersey | 6 | 6 | 6 | 6 |
| New Mexico | 4 | 6 | 6 | 4 |
| New York | 6 | 6 | 6 | 6 |

| State | Oral | Written | Promissory | Open |
|---|---|---|---|---|
| North Carolina | 3 | 3 | 5 | 3 |
| North Dakota | 6 | 6 | 6 | 6 |
| Ohio | 6 | 15 | 15 | 6 |
| Oklahoma | 3 | 5 | 5 | 3 |
| Oregon | 6 | 6 | 6 | 6 |
| Pennsylvania | 4 | 4 | 4 | 4 |
| Rhode Island | 15 | 15 | 10 | 10 |
| South Carolina | 3 | 3 | 3 | 3 |
| South Dakota | 3 | 6 | 6 | 6 |
| Tennessee | 6 | 6 | 6 | 6 |
| Texas | 4 | 4 | 4 | 4 |
| Utah | 4 | 6 | 6 | 4 |
| Vermont | 6 | 6 | 5 | 3 |
| Virginia | 3 | 5 | 6 | 3 |
| Washington | 3 | 6 | 6 | 3 |
| West Virginia | 5 | 10 | 6 | 5 |
| Wisconsin | 6 | 6 | 10 | 6 |
| Wyoming | 8 | 10 | 10 | 8 |

# Notes

# Re-Aging a Delinquent Account

Positive re-aging is designed to help customers who are making an effort to get back on their feet after financial problems. Once you fall behind on a bill, it can be difficult to catch up. Unless you can come up with a large lump sum to pay off your debt , your account may be reported as late every month, even though you are making some payments. When this happens, it's called "rolling lates." To prevent these types of accounts from being listed as delinquent every month, the bank or card issuer can re-age them so they are reported as current.

In this type of re-aging, an account that was reported as late each month to the credit reporting agencies will now be reported as "paid on time." Sometimes the financial institution will go back into the past payment history and bring all the delinquent payments current. In other cases, the account will simply be listed as "paid on time" for the current month and going forward, as long as payments continue to be made on time.

**Many lenders are willing to help customers who:**

- Have a long-standing record of payment
- Are able to repay past due balances
- Have made at least three consecutive payments on time since the discrepancy

# How to request Positive Re-Aging

Contact your creditor and request they re-age your account. You should have a plan of action prior to contacting them of how you are going to tackle the debt.

# Notes

# Adding the home you rent to your credit report

There are 3rd party companies that will add rental history to your credit report. The cost will be charged to you and not the landlord or property management company

## The companies are:

**Rental Kharma** – Rental Kharma will report 24 month history to your Transunion report only. The tenants do not have to pay rent to a 3rd party. Instead, their landlord will provide verification of on time payment to Rental Kharma.

**RentBureau** - Receives updated rental payment data from property management companies and electronic rent payment services & reports to Experian. If you rent from an individual landlord or property management company that does not report data, sign up through a rent payment service working with RentBureau.

**RentTrack** – RentTrack is the only company that reports to All 3 Bureaus. Sign up to pay your rent to rent track and they will deposit your rent to your landlords account and you can opt-in to credit reporting.

**Rent Reporters** – Will report your rent to Transunion. You should see an update to your credit report in as little as 15 days

# Notes

# 12 Credit Mistakes

## Things that will negatively impact your score

- Close a credit card, especially an older one – The longer your credit history is, the higher your scores will be. An aged credit card with an excellent payment history and low balance is the BEST credit card.

- Pay an old collection that hasn't reported in over 2 years. This causes the bureaus to begin reporting the debt currently and thus bring your scores down. Although it is a paid collection, it's still a collection nonetheless

- Take out a payday loan or become delinquent on one. Payday loans are predatory loans that have exorbitant interest rates

- Apply for multiple accounts (excluding car or mortgage) causing numerous inquiries – Multiple inquiries will drop your score

- Pay your bills 30 days late.

- Go over your credit card limit – Even when you pay down balance, the fact that you went above your limit will always appear on your report, and have a negative impact your score

- ~~Court judgment, tax lien, bankruptcies, and other legal punishments will carry an additional negative penalty, especially when they are recent.~~ As of July 1, 2017, these items will no longer appear on your credit report. This is great news! However, just because they no longer appear on your credit report, it does not alleviate your responsibility. These items may still pop up when you are trying to purchase a home.

- Having a P.O. Box listed as your address or having multiple addresses.
- Having your occupation stated on credit report is a possible risk.
- Having accounts listed as ‘Closed by credit grantor’ or closed by the lending institution.
- Paying a credit card to 0 and not utilizing it for an extended period of time.
- Disputing old items that haven’t reported in several years can cause a creditor to begin reporting current and collection efforts may begin

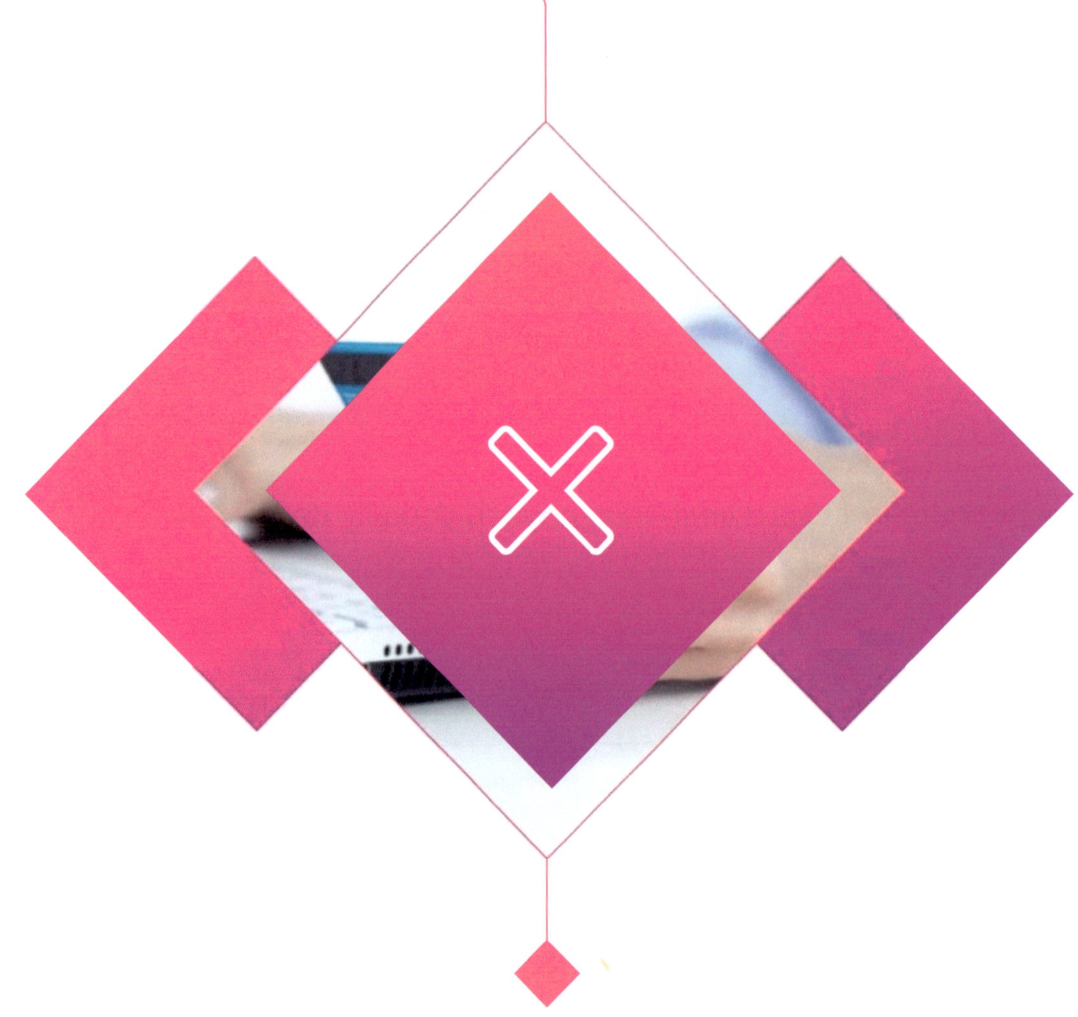

# Notes

## Tips to paying off multiple credit card accounts

1. Pay off the card with the highest interest rate
2. Pay as much as you can above minimum payment
3. Pay before the due date
4. Request an interest rate reduction
5. Once you knock down that card, go to the next one.

*If you can get a credit increase on the lowest interest rate card and transfer the balance there, that would help significantly.*

## Tips to paying off your mortgage quicker

1. Bi-weekly payment – If you pay your mortgage bi-weekly, it essentially gives you one extra payment per year and saves you about 4 years on your mortgage
2. Pay an extra mortgage payment per quarter (every 4 months) and you can save up to 11 years on your mortgage payment

*Each method will save you thousands of dollars of interest, but be sure to consult with your mortgage company to ensure they are applying your extra payments to principal*

# Notes

## Establishing Credit After Bankruptcy

*It is extremely important to re-establish your credit after bankruptcy. Allowing your credit to lay dormant is one of the worse things you can do. Having a mixture of credit accounts is also very important to establishing great credit scores*

Tips to re-establish after bankruptcy

1. Open a couple of credit card accounts immediately
2. Add your rental history to your credit report
3. If you do not have a car, get one
4. Purchase a home

## Purchasing a home after Bankruptcy

*Purchasing a home after Bankruptcy is very attainable if you have successfully re-established your credit. Here are the timeframes of when you can purchase a home after bankruptcy*

1. VA Loan – 2 years
2. FHA Loan – 2 years
3. Conventional Loan – 4 years

# Notes

## Student Loans

Student loans can have simultaneously a negative and positive impact on your credit. If you pay your student loans on time, it can help increase your score significantly. It's imperative to keep student loans in good standing, as it is one of the few debts that is nearly impossible to get rid of without paying off. You live with them darn near until you die, or until they are paid in full.. whichever comes first.

Question: How do they hurt? Answer: Your debt to income ratio. One of the saddest things I run across is a person making $40k per year with over $200k in student loans. If they are in deferment, lenders are required to use 1% of the student loan balance as a monthly payment. So for a $200k loan, you are hit with a $2,000 per month payment. If you are not in deferment, we hit you with the actual payment. Think about this, at $40k per year, your gross monthly income is $3,300. If we are taking $2,000 out of your qualifying income, you only qualify with $1,300, that's IF you have no other debt. If you are getting FHA financing, that means you only qualify for a payment of up to $650. That's roughly about $100k.

# Student Loan Forgiveness

There are a few instances that student loan debt can be cancelled or forgiven. They are

01 School Closure - You may be eligible for a 100% discharge of your Direct Loans, Federal Family Education Loan (FFEL) Program loans, or Federal Perkins Loans under either of these circumstances:

- Your school closes while you're enrolled, and you do not complete your program because of the closure. If you were on an approved leave of absence, you are considered to have been enrolled at the school.
- Your school closes within 120 days after you withdraw.

02 Public Service Forgiveness - If you are employed by a government or not-for-profit organization, you may be able to receive loan forgiveness under the Public Service Loan Forgiveness Program .

03 Teacher Forgiveness - The Teacher Loan Forgiveness Program is intended to encourage individuals to enter and continue in the teaching profession. Under this program, if you teach full-time for five complete and consecutive academic years in certain elementary and secondary schools and educational service agencies that serve low-income families, and meet other qualifications, you may be eligible for forgiveness of up to a combined total of $17,500 on your Direct Subsidized and Unsubsidized Loans and your Subsidized and Unsubsidized Federal Stafford Loans. If you have Plus Loans only , you are not eligible for this type of forgiveness.

04 Perkins Loan Cancellation & Discharge - Applies to individuals who perform certain types of public service or are employed in certain occupations including Peace Corp, Teachers, Armed Forces, Nurse or Medical Tech, Law Enforcement or Corrections, Head start Worker, Child or Family Service Worker, Early Intervention Service Provider

05 Total & Permanent Disability Discharge - A total and permanent disability (TPD) discharge relieves you from having to repay a William D. Ford Federal Direct Loan (Direct Loan) Program loan, Federal Family Education Loan (FFEL) Program loan, and/or Federal Perkins Loan (Perkins Loan) Program loan or complete a Teacher Education Assistance for College and Higher Education (TEACH) Grant service obligation on the basis of your total and permanent disability.

06 Discharge due to death

07 Discharge due to bankruptcy (rare) - You may have your federal student loan discharged in chapter 7 or chapter 13 bankruptcy only if you file a separate action, known as an "adversary proceeding," requesting the bankruptcy court find that repayment would impose undue hardship on you and your dependents.

08 False Certification of Student Eligibility or Unauthorized Payment Discharge - You may be eligible for a discharge of your Direct Loan or FFEL Program loan in these circumstances:

- Your school falsely certified your eligibility to receive the loan based on your ability to benefit from its training, and you did not meet the ability to benefit student eligibility requirements.
- The school signed your name on the application or promissory note without your authorization or the school endorsed your loan check or signed your authorization for electronic funds transfer without your knowledge, unless the proceeds of the loan were delivered to you or applied to charges owed by you to the school.
- Your loan was falsely certified because you were a victim of identity theft.
- The school certified your eligibility, but because of a physical or mental condition, age, criminal record, or other reason you are disqualified from employment in the occupation in which you were being trained.

09 Unpaid Refund Discharge - You may be eligible for a discharge of your Direct Loan or FFEL Program loan if you withdrew from school, but the school didn’t pay a refund that it owed to the U.S. Department of Education or to the lender

10 Borrower Defense Application - Borrowers may be eligible for forgiveness of the federal student loans used to attend a school if that school misled them or engaged in other misconduct in violation of certain laws.

# Removing Student Loan Late Payments

Student loans are a tough nut to crack once you become delinquent. Since you are required to have special circumstances for them to be forgiven, most people end up being stuck with them for most of their lives. The good news is only 7% of all student loans nationwide are delinquent, the bad news (for me at least) is 70% of the credit reports that have student loans that come across my desk have been delinquent at some point. There is a way that the late payments can be removed. Send a Goodwill letter to your student loan servicing company after you have made at least 6-12 consecutive on time payments. The letter should be very positive simple, and to the point. If you have any documentation to support hardship that you may include that as well. This letter should be faxed & emailed to all student loan companies you had delinquencies with.

## Sample Goodwill Letter

Date:

Name & Address:

Phone:

Student Loan Company Name & Address

Acct#:

To whom it may concern,

Thank you for taking the time to read my letter. I am writing regarding late payments on my credit report for the months of (dates). During this time, I faced (description of hardship) that impacted my ability to make payments. As you may have noticed, I have been making on time payments every month since (month) for the past (how many months/years). I am currently applying for a home mortgage and the late payments have negatively impacted my ability to qualify. It would help greatly if you would be willing to allow a goodwill adjustment to remove all late payments from my credit file.

Thank you for your consideration,

Signature

# Notes

# Budgeting for a home

There are many down payment assistance programs offered by various Cities, Counties, States, Governmental, and Private entities. Some require repayment, others are grants that you do not have to pay back. But all of them have certain criteria and guidelines that must be followed. Whether its income, neighborhood, household, or employment restrictions, everyone does not fit into the down payment assistance box. For those who do not, it means you must save. 70% of Americans do not have a budget in writing, and if you do not have a budget, it may not be an easy task to save for a home

## *There are several sources you can use for down payment*

### *Your Tax Return*

You've overpaid Uncle Sam, and now it's time to reap your reward. For a home that's $100k, you need a minimum of $3000 for down payment

### *Your 401k*

You joined the company Retirement plan, and your employer has matched your contribution, now you have a nice kitty you put away for retirement. **There are stipulations that you may borrow from your 401k with minimum penalties, as long as it is to purchase a home**

### *A Gift from a friend or family member*

Your rich Aunt decided to bless you with a gift to purchase a home

### *The Rent-to-Mortgage savings method (page 53)*

You take the difference between your potential mortgage payment & your current rent and begin saving every month. This will not only help you save quite a bit for down payment, but will prepare & discipline you for a higher monthly housing expense

If you have none of the options listed, then you will have to buckle down and save for your down payment yourself. Depending on how well you do, it may take as little as a few months, or a maybe a couple of years. If you are disciplined, you can totally pull it off.

Now it's time to get your pen and calculator so we can figure out how long it will take you to save for a down payment:

## How much mortgage can you afford?

### Your Gross Monthly Income

$

### Your Gross Monthly Income

| | |
|---|---|
| Car Payment(s) | $ |
| Personal loan(s) | $ |
| Minimum Credit Card Payment(s) | $ |
| **Total Debt** | $ |

## SUBTRACT your Total Debt from your Gross Monthly Income

| | |
|---|---|
| **Gross Monthly Income** | $ |
| **Total Debt** | $ |
| **Net Qualifying Amount** | = |

## MULTIPLY your Net Qualifying Amount by 45%

| | |
|---|---|
| **Net Qualifying Amount** | $ |
| **Multiply by 45%** | ____________ X45%<br>(or x .45) |

*Total FHA Mortgage Payment* (This is approximately the amount of payment you can likely qualify for. Please note, it can vary slightly depending on your credit score. If your score is 640 or above multiple by 55%. If your score is less than 620, multiply by 40%)

# How much home you can afford?

Diagram G

| Purchase Price | Down Payment | FHA Payments |
|---|---|---|
| $ 100,000.00 | $ 3,500.00 | $ 653.79 |
| $ 150,000.00 | $ 5,250.00 | $ 980.68 |
| $ 200,000.00 | $ 7,000.00 | $ 1,307.58 |
| $ 250,000.00 | $ 8,750.00 | $ 1,634.47 |
| $ 300,000.00 | $ 10,500.00 | $ 1,961.37 |
| $ 350,000.00 | $ 12,250.00 | $ 2,288.26 |
| $ 400,000.00 | $ 14,000.00 | $ 2,615.16 |
| $ 450,000.00 | $ 15,750.00 | $ 2,942.05 |
| $ 500,000.00 | $ 17,500.00 | $ 3,268.94 |
| $ 550,000.00 | $ 19,250.00 | $ 3,595.84 |
| $ 600,000.00 | $ 21,000.00 | $ 3,992.73 |
| $ 625,500.00 | $ 21,892.50 | $ 4,089.51 |

Payments are based upon a 4% APR. Taxes & insurance are included. Please note, final payments may vary depending on the interest rate, tax base, and insurance as they may differ per location.

# How long will it take to save for a down payment?

The Rent-to-mortgage savings method (Described on page 59)

See Diagram G

Determine the amount you qualify for $ __________

Down payment amount $ __________

Current monthly rent $ __________

Subtract the Mortgage payment from the current rent amount

(Example: for $250k purchase price & rent $1,000 per month)

$1634.47 - $1000 = $634.47 (the amount of money you save monthly)

Monthly savings $ __________

Amount saved in 12 months $ __________

# How long will it take to save for a down payment?

## The Income Percentage Method

See Diagram G

| | |
|---|---|
| Total Qualifying Mortgage Payment | |
| Your Purchase Price | |
| Your Down Payment Needed | |

Your Gross Monthly Income x 10% per month (If you can afford more replace the 10% with the percentage of your income you can realistically afford to save)

| | |
|---|---|
| Gross Monthly Income | $ |
| Multiply by 10% | ______ X10%<br>(or x .10) |
| Gross Monthly Income | $ |
| Multiply by 10% | ______ X10%<br>(or x .10) |

Total Savings Per Month

# Notes

# Resources

# Courtesy Late Removal

Your Name & Address

Collector's Name & Address

Date

Re: Account Number XXXX-XXXX-XXXX-XXXX

Dear (Credit Card Company),

I am writing to request that you would remove the late payment on my credit card (account listed above) for the month(s) of (month/year). As you can see, I have had this credit card for (number) years and It has remained in good standing until (event took place).

Please send your response via email at (email address), by fax (fax number) or to my home address listed above.

Thank you for your consideration

# Re-Aging

Your Name & Address

Collector's Name & Address

Date

Re: Account Number XXXX-XXXX-XXXX-XXXX

Dear Collection Manager:

I am requesting that you positively re-age my account referenced above. I have made payments on (date) to bring the account current. I have had (explain hardship) and I am now in a position to make on-time payments going forward. However, the late payments reflecting on my credit report are hurting my credit score drastically and impeding my ability to make a major purchase like buying a home.

Please send your response via email at (email address), by fax (fax number) or to my home address listed above.

Thank you for your consideration

# Removing Aliases

Your Name & Address

Collector's Name & Address

Date

Re: Account Number XXXX-XXXX-XXXX-XXXX
Re: Correction of erroneous/inaccurate information in my consumer credit file/report.

Dear (Credit Bureau):
I just recently received a copy of my credit report and noticed outdated and incorrect personal information in my file. Please see my license that I have attached and update my credit file to only reflect my name, (Your Name), my birthday (DOB), and my current address (Your Address). Please provide a copy of my report with the updated information as soon as possible
Thank you,
Signature

# Removing Inquiries

Your Name & Address

Collector's Name & Address

Date
Re: Removal of erroneous inquiries from my credit file

Dear (Credit Bureau):
I reviewed a copy of my credit report and (Company Name) ran an unauthorized credit inquiry (Date)
I never authorized such action and this constitutes a violation of my rights under the Fair Credit Reporting Act §604 as well as a violation of my rights to privacy. Please investigate this occurrence and respond back in writing immediately.
If you have any questions or need additional information, please contact me at address listed above.

Thank you,
Signature

# Debt Validation

Date:
Name: & Address:
Phone:
Collection Agency: & Address:
Acct#:

I am writing this letter in response to the phone call/letter received from you on (Date). In conformance to my rights under the Fair Debt Collection Practices Act (FDCPA), I am requesting you to provide me with a validation of the debt that you talked of earlier. Please note, this a not a refusal to pay, rather a statement that your claim is disputed and validation is demanded. (15 USC 1692g Sec. 809 (b))
I do hereby request that your office provide me with complete documentation to verify that I owe the said debt and have any legal obligation to pay you.
Please provide me with the following:
Agreement with the creditor that authorizes you to collect on this alleged debt
The agreement bearing my signature stating that I have agreed to assume the debt
Valid copies of the debt agreement stating the amount of the debt and interest charges
Proof that the Statute of Limitations has not expired

# Debt Validation Cont'd

Complete payment history on this account along with an accounting of all additional charges being assessed
Show me that you are licensed to collect in my state; and
Your license numbers and Registered Agent
If your office fails to reply to this debt validation letter within 30 days from the date of your receipt, all instances related to this account must be immediately deleted and completely removed from my credit file. Moreover, all future attempts to collect on the said debt must be ceased.
Your non-compliance with my request will also be construed as an absolute waiver of all claims to enforce the debt against me and your implied agreement to compensate me for court costs and attorney fees if I am forced to bring this matter before a judge.
Thank you,
Your Signature

# Failure to Validate

Date:
Name: & Address:
Phone:
Collection Agency: & Address:
Acct#:
Re: Removal of erroneous inquiries from my credit file

Dear (Credit Bureau):
I reviewed a copy of my credit report and (Company Name) ran an unauthorized credit inquiry (Date)
I never authorized such action and this constitutes a violation of my rights under the Fair Credit Reporting Act §604 as well as a violation of my rights to privacy. Please investigate this occurrence and respond back in writing immediately.
If you have any questions or need additional information, please contact me at address listed above.

Thank you,
Signature

# Debt Settlement

Name & Address

Collector's Name & Address

Date

Re: Account Number XXXX-XXXX-XXXX-XXXX

This letter is in response to your call/letter/credit report entry on (date) for the account referenced above. I would like to pay off or settle this debt in full and save both of our time and efforts.
I'd like to clarify that I am not acknowledging or accepting that I owe this debt. I respectfully request that you properly verify your right to collect on this debt, in addition to providing me with an accounting of the amount I owe. I am aware that your company can report the debt to the credit bureaus as necessary and that you have the ability to change the account status since you are the information provider.
I hope you'll also agree to not discuss this offer with any third party (except the original creditor). If you find my offer acceptable, please send me a letter agreeing to these terms, signed by your authorized representative, and subject to the laws of my state.
Under the Fair Debt Collection Practices Act, I have the right to dispute this alleged debt. If I do not receive your postmarked response within the next 15 business days, I shall withdraw my offer.
Please forward your agreement to my address listed above.
Sincerely,

# Debt Settlement Counter offer

Date:
Name: & Address:
Phone:
Collection Agency: & Address:
Acct#:
Re: Removal of erroneous inquiries from my credit file

I appreciate that your company is willing to work with me in settling my debt so that I may pay it off. This letter is to make a counter offer in response to the settlement offer made by your company, which I received on Date

The amount that I propose to settle the debt in full is ($dollar amount) I would also like to request that you remove any late payments or charge-offs on this account from my credit report.

I have several debt accounts that I am attempting to settle as well. Unfortunately, I have a limited amount of funds. So, I can only pay those creditors who are willing to meet my terms. I have already reached several mutually agreeable settlements with other creditors, and I doubt that I'll have enough funds to pay everyone.

If your company is willing to accept my proposal, please sign the attached letter agreeing to my proposal and return a copy to me. As soon as I receive this signed acknowledged agreement, I shall send you a money order in the amount I've proposed.

Sincerely,

# Pay for Deletion

Date:
Name: & Address:
Phone:
Collection Agency: & Address:
Acct#:

Re: Account Number XXXX-XXXX-XXXX-XXXX

Dear Collection Manager:
This letter is in response to your (letter / call / credit report entry) on (date) related to the debt referenced above. I wish to save us both some time and effort by settling this debt.
Please be aware that this is not an acknowledgment or acceptance of the debt, as I have not received any verification of the debt. Nor is this a promise to pay and is not a payment agreement unless you provide a response as detailed below.
I am aware that your company can report this debt to the credit bureaus as you deem necessary.
Furthermore, you can change the listing since you are the information furnisher.

# Pay for Deletion cont'd

I am willing to pay (this debt in full / $XXX as settlement for this debt) in return for your agreement to remove all information regarding this debt from the credit reporting agencies within ten calendar days of payment.

If you agree to the terms, I will send certified payment in the amount of $XXX payable to (Collection Agency) in exchange to have all information related to this debt removed from all of my credit files.

If you accept this offer, you also agree not to discuss the offer with any third-party, excluding the original creditor. If you accept the offer, please prepare a letter on your company letterhead agreeing to the terms. This letter should be signed by an authorized agent of (Collection Agency). The letter will be treated as a contract and subject to the laws of my state.

As granted by the Fair Debt Collection Practices Act, I have the right to dispute this alleged debt. If I do not receive your postmarked response within 15 days, I will withdraw the offer and request full verification of this debt.

Please forward your agreement to the address listed above.

Sincerely,

# Statue of Limitations

Date:
Name: & Address:
Phone:
Collection Agency: & Address:
Acct#:

Re: Account Number XXXX-XXXX-XXXX-XXXX
This letter is in response to your communication dated (date) regarding the collection on the debt account referenced above

I do not believe that I owe this debt, and therefore dispute this account. I am aware of my rights under the Fair Debt Collection Practices Act (FDCPA) and my state laws. I have checked with my State's Attorney General and verified that the Statute of Limitations for this type of debt in [state in which the contract was signed] has expired. If you intend to take this issue to court, I shall inform the court that I have disputed this debt and that the Statute of Limitations has expired.

Neither you nor anyone affiliated to your company should contact me except to inform me that collection efforts are terminated or that you or the creditor are taking specific actions allowed by the FDCPA and my state's law.

I shall consider any other contact a violation of The Fair Debt Collection Practices Act and will report it immediately to my State's Attorney General and the Federal Trade Commission. Please be advised that I keep a log of all phone calls and any violation of the FDCPA can result in your company being fined up to $1000 per violation.
Sincerely,

# Student Loan Goodwill Letter

Date:
Name & Address:
Phone:
Student Loan Company Name & Address
Acct#:

To whom it may concern,
Thank you for taking the time to read my letter. I am writing regarding late payments on my credit report for the months of (dates). During this time, I faced (description of hardship) that impacted my ability to make payments. As you may have noticed, I have been making on time payments every month since (month) for the past (how many months/years). I am currently applying for a home mortgage and the late payments have negatively impacted my ability to qualify. It would help greatly if you would be willing to allow a goodwill adjustment to remove all late payments from my credit file.
Thank you for your consideration,
Signature

# Dispute Letter

Your Name & Address

Collector's Name & Address

Date

Re: Account Number XXXX-XXXX-XXXX-XXXX

Re: Correction of erroneous/inaccurate information in my consumer credit file/report.

Dear (Credit Bureau):
I just recently received a copy of my credit report and noticed a number of outdated and incorrect information in my file. Please begin an immediate investigation of the following items listed below in my credit report. Please address the following items immediately and send me an updated corrected copy of my report at the conclusion of your investigation.

1. Account disputes
a. Aurora Bank FSB Acct xxxx – this was not a foreclosure, this was included in my bankruptcy
b. Bank of America Acct#xxx – This is not my account
c. Homeward Residential #xxxx– This is not my account
2. The following AKA/Alias information should be deleted from my credit profile as they are not valid/accurate
a. Name Aliases that should be removed
3. The following addresses should be deleted from my credit profile as they are not valid/accurate
a. List all addresses other than your current that appears on your credit report
Thank you for your help and prompt attention to this matter
Your Name & Signature

# Re: Request to provide method of verification

Date:
Credit Bureau Name & Address
Your Name, Address Social & DOB

To Whom It May Concern: On [Insert Original Dispute Date] I requested an investigation because I felt the item is not being reported legally, and on [Insert Date of Response] I received a letter stating that your investigation was complete. Please answer the following questions: What certified documents were reviewed to conclude your investigation? Please provide me a complete copy of all of the information that was transmitted to the data furnisher as part of the investigation, as required by FCRA: · Who did you speak with? · What was the date? · How long was the conversation? · What was their position? · What number did you call? · What is the name of your employee that spoke directly to the creditor? · What is the position of your employee that spoke to the creditor? This inaccurate reporting has caused me severe financial and emotional distress. Please reply within 15 days to the above questions, or delete the items.
Sincerely,

Your name

# NOTICE OF INTENT TO FILE COMPLAINT

Date:
Credit Bureau Name & Address
Your Name, Address Social & DOB
RE: Follow-up Dispute Letter of (insert date of original validation request letter)

To Whom It May Concern: This letter shall serve as formal notice of my intent to file a complaint with the FTC, due to your disregard of the law. You claim to have somehow verified the items I requested. Therefore, I legally requested a description of the procedures used to verify the information. As indicated by the attached copy of the letter and mailing receipt [Insert Date on Receipt], you received and accepted through registered mail my request letter dated [Insert Date of Your Letter]. To date you have not responded to this request and have thus not performed your duty mentioned in the law. Federal law requires you to respond within 15 days, yet you have failed to respond and it has been over 30 days. Failure to comply with these federal regulations by credit reporting agencies is investigated by the Federal Trade Commission (see 15 USC 41, et seq.). I am maintaining a careful record of my communications with you on this matter; for the purpose of filing a complaint with the FTC, unless I hear from you in 20 days. For the record, the following information is being erroneously included on my credit report. [List all company name( s) and account number( s)] You claimed to have verified the erroneous information, yet you refuse to tell me HOW you were able to verify these accounts. If you do not immediately remove this inaccurate and/ or incomplete information, I will file a formal complaint with the FTC. As I stated, I am carefully documenting these events, including the lack of response REQUIRED under federal law from you. Any further delay is inexcusable.

Sincerely,

Your Name

# Notes

# Notes

# Notes

CONSTANCE
CARTER

Made in the USA
Columbia, SC
28 April 2025

56972005R00066